Be Brave, Little Elephant

**CARING FOR ANIMALS AT OMAHA'S
HENRY DOORLY ZOO & AQUARIUM**

BY CAROL BICAK

**PHOTOS BY CHRIS MACHIAN AND KENT SIEVERS
OF THE OMAHA WORLD-HERALD**

Emmet is Annie's stuffed elephant.
She loves him and takes good care of him.
But her silly dog thought he was a chew toy. The dog tore
Emmet's right ear and bit his leg before Annie could rescue him.

Now Emmet is scared, because Annie is taking him to the
teddy bear hospital at Omaha's Henry Doorly Zoo.
Doctors! Needles! Operations! Oh, no!

Emmet wants to shout,
"I'm not a teddy bear! I'm an elephant!" That's OK.
This hospital is for any stuffed toy that needs mending.

At the zoo they find a long line at the teddy bear hospital.
Emmet is just one of lots of hurt toys. Annie asks her mom
if they can walk around the zoo. "Awesome!" Emmet thinks.
"Maybe we'll walk so long, the hospital will close."

When they get to Lemur Walkway, the little elephant is surprised when a
red-ruffed lemur named Red hops over and whispers, "I want to be friends."
Emmet needs a friend. He tells the lemur he is afraid to go to the hospital.
Red says the animals aren't afraid, because they have learned
the zoo doctors and staff only want to help them.

Emmet and Annie watch the lemurs receive care.
One had an eye operation and needs eyedrops. Another gets a shot.
A gray ring-tailed lemur named Rhea hops on the scale.
She has a disease called diabetes that won't ever go away, so she has to take
special medicine. She shows Emmet her tail, which got hurt.
It has a bandage, because it takes a long time for her to heal.
"It's not so bad," Rhea says. "Be brave."

At Bear Canyon, Emmet sees two playful Andean bears.
"When we first came to the zoo, we were overweight," one named Freckles
tells Emmet. "We had to eat a special diet to lose a few pounds."
The other bear, Ditka, says, "And we had to exercise to get in shape."
Emmet can see they are healthy bears now. "Be brave," Freckles says.
"The doctors want to make you healthy, too."

Emmet thinks a snow leopard named Pasha looks dangerous,
but he turns out to be just a big pussycat. He purrs that the big cats
often need shots. "Needles sound bad," Pasha says,
"but after a quick prick in our tails, we hardly feel a thing."
Sometimes zoo dentists check the big cats' teeth,
but only after giving them medicine to make them sleep.
"They don't want us to bite their hands by accident!"

In the Desert Dome, Emmet meets a springhaas named Nettles,

who looks like a rabbit with a long tail.

She broke a leg and had to go to the zoo hospital.

It was a little scary being away from her family,

but the doctors were kind, and her broken leg healed.

"Be brave," Nettles says to Emmet.

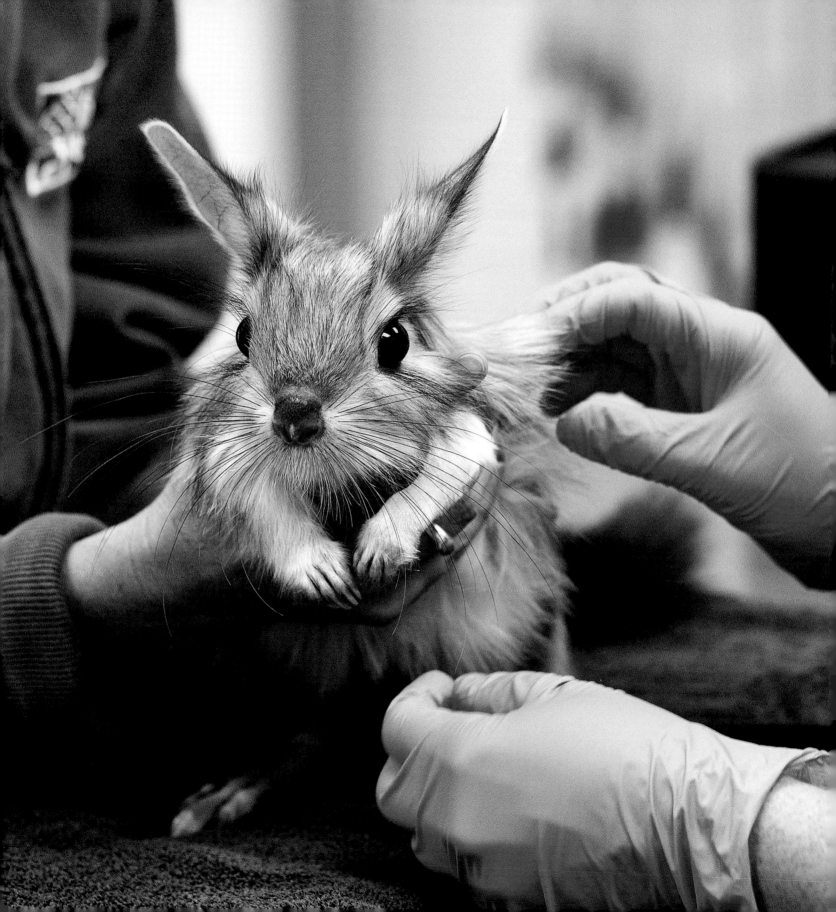

Annie and Emmet can't help smiling at the silly meerkats.
Some stand as still as statues. Others chase each other and act like
they are fighting. They tell Emmet they are trained to hop in their crates
so the zookeepers don't have to spend all day trying to catch them
for their annual checkups and shots. "Be brave," they squeak.

At Gorilla Valley, Emmet and Annie see Mo, a big silverback gorilla
who needs his heart tested. "I come close to the doctors
so they can take pictures of my heart," Mo tells Emmet.
The doctors are trying to find a cure for heart disease in gorillas.
"Be brave," Mo says. "They're not trying to hurt you."

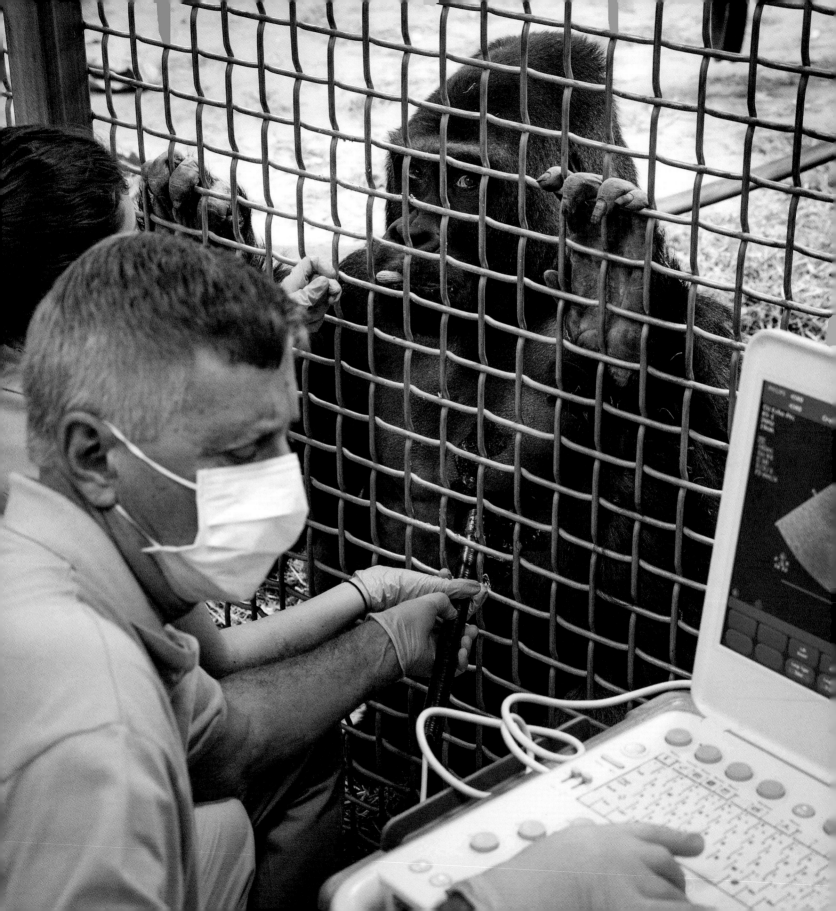

Annie's mom next takes them to the aquarium to see the beautiful fish,
who have their own stories. They tell Emmet that when
they first came to the zoo, they had to stay separated from other fish.
"They didn't want us to spread any sickness in the tanks,"
says a pretty orange fish named Lucy. "Once they were sure
we were healthy, we got to join the others."

Emmet is startled when a big loggerhead turtle swims up.
Harold is 20 years old, and sometimes he isn't a good patient.
He has to be taken out of the tank and over to the hospital once a year for his
checkup and a special picture called an X-ray. It's hard to be weighed when
you're a 280-pound turtle. The trip to the hospital makes Harold cranky,
not scared. "There's nothing to be scared of," he tells Emmet. "So be brave."

Annie and Emmet make their way to Pachyderm Hill,
where they find Fitz, an Indian rhinoceros who loves to take mud baths.
They see his legs have a rash that might be an allergy.
Fitz tells Emmet the doctors won't give up looking for a cause and a cure.
"Be brave, little elephant.
Doctors never stop trying to find out what is wrong.'"

Annie is getting tired, so she asks her mom to take them back
to the Teddy Bear Hospital. They hop on the Skyfari and fly over the zoo.
The ride takes Emmet's mind off the hospital.
When they get off, they spy the giraffes. One of them, Jawara,
tells Emmet he has been trained to put his head down for X-rays.
The pictures show zoo doctors how to treat Jawara's teeth.
"Don't worry, little elephant," he says. "Doctors make you feel better."

When Emmet finally arrives at the teddy bear hospital,
he thinks about all the things he has learned from the animals at the zoo.
Doctors and dentists are nice and don't give up on finding answers.
Shots and tests may be uncomfortable, but the hurt doesn't last.
Doctors' tools may look frightening, but they help find what is wrong.

"I'm going to be brave," Emmet thinks. And he is.
When he wakes up in the teddy bear hospital, his ear and his leg
are as good as new, and he's ready to go home.

Animal care and training at Omaha's Henry Doorly Zoo & Aquarium

Omaha's Henry Doorly Zoo & Aquarium faces a huge job in providing for the welfare of more than 57,000 animals. Gone are the days when zookeepers had to act like cowboys, chasing and lassoing running animals or shooting tranquilizer darts. The animals now are trained to present themselves for shots or exams, which helps them stay calm and to be comfortable with the procedures the staff must perform.

Training is not just for lions and tigers and bears, but also for sharks, alligators, lemurs, giraffes, rhinos and gorillas. And for zookeepers. Zoo personnel learn to use positive reinforcement, not punishment, for animals that don't cooperate or are slow to catch on. "We don't make an animal do anything," said Jay Pratte, coordinator of animal training.

Jay Pratte

The trick is to find out what an animal likes and then offer it as a reward. The likes can be food. Big cats like meat, of course, but who knew a polar bear would crave celery? Other animals like something else entirely. The white rhinos, for example, like to have their skin scrubbed.

Giraffes love leafy vegetables as a treat. The trainer feeds this giraffe to get it in place for a head X-ray.

The training starts out slowly. "Little behaviors lead to big ones," Pratte said. The result is less stress for the animals and the humans. "We build trust. It helps when the animals know what to do." Each animal is treated as an individual, working on its own time frame. Some learn by just watching one another.

The trainers use different signals to direct animals. Sharks head for a target ball. Some animals, such as lemurs, react to clickers. Others follow whistles.

In training, animals respond well to rewards. Meat is a great reward for big cats.

Zebra sharks love yellow objects and swim toward that color.

Trainers often receive unexpected rewards. Snow leopards are known to be reclusive and cautious, Pratte said. When they come out and cooperate, it is a sign of the trust that has built up with their trainers. Trainers also face hazards. But bites and knockdowns don't discourage them.

Trust between the animals and their trainers is the most important aspect of the program. Some treatments hurt or are stressful. "You can't tell an animal, 'This is good for you,'" Pratte said. The animal has to learn that a procedure — from hoof trimming to X-rays to shots — isn't so bad after all.

This aardvark enjoys pomegranate-flavored yogurt. She is getting an ultrasound.

Omaha's Henry Doorly Zoo & Aquarium animal health staff

The staff of Omaha's Henry Doorly Zoo & Aquarium maintains the good health of more than 1,300 species. Medical needs include regular physicals, dental exams and vaccinations, plus treating injuries and illnesses. The zoo's efforts also are aimed at stabilizing or increasing the numbers of species.

Zoo vets can encounter unusual situations. For example, a shark had to have a fin amputated after she was injured by an aggressive male. The doctors also may be called on to seek the cause of a rhino's skin irritation. Or figure out the best way to treat a giraffe's dental disease. Or work with other zoos to discover why so many male gorillas have heart disease. Some of their work results in great moments, like saving the life of a fragile newborn lion cub.

Dr. Doug Armstrong is the zoo's director of animal health. His staff includes fellow veterinarians Julie Napier, Christina Ploog, Jennifer Waldoch and Stephanie Carle. The medical facilities are located in the Grewcock Center for Conservation and Research, which opened in 1996.

The zoo also provides care for stuffed animals at its popular Teddy Bear Weekend. Children can bring their toys for checkups and, if necessary, a visit to the emergency room. Emmet highly recommends the event.

Omaha's Henry Doorly Zoo & Aquarium

In 2014, travel website TripAdvisor named Omaha's Henry Doorly Zoo & Aquarium the world's best zoo in its Travelers' Choice awards. The attraction has come a long way from its beginnings as Riverside Park, a city park founded in 1894. The park's menagerie grew, and the Omaha Zoological Society was organized in 1952 to help improve conditions for the animal collection. In 1963, Margaret Hitchcock Doorly donated $750,000 to the zoo with the stipulation that the zoo be named for her late husband, Henry Doorly, publisher of The World-Herald. The zoological society in 1965 was reorganized to run the zoo as a nonprofit organization.

Dennis Pate
Zoo Director and CEO

The Cat Complex, one of the largest in North America, opened in 1977. The zoo continued to grow in the 1980s and 1990s, adding such attractions as Mutual of Omaha's Wild Kingdom Pavilion, Lied Jungle, Scott Aquarium and the Lozier IMAX Theater. Most of this growth was overseen by Dr. Lee "Doc" Simmons, its widely respected director from 1970 to 2009. Other exhibits have followed, including the Desert Dome, Kingdoms of the Night and Expedition Madagascar. Current Director and CEO Dennis Pate has envisioned a master plan that calls for a total redesign of the zoo over the next decade or so.

You may have noticed that Emmet didn't meet any real elephants in the story. Henry Doorly's only elephant, Shenga, was sent to the zoo in Columbus, Ohio, so she wouldn't be alone. The move left the Omaha zoo elephantless. But work has begun on the largest project in the zoo's history — an outdoor grasslands habitat for African wildlife that will include the addition of a herd of elephants. The zoo remains committed to its animals and to the education about conservation of our natural treasures. It is an accredited member of the Association of Zoos and Aquariums and participates in its species survival plans.

BE BRAVE, LITTLE ELEPHANT
BY CAROL BICAK

PHOTOS BY
CHRIS MACHIAN & KENT SIEVERS

EDITOR
Dan Sullivan

DESIGNER
Christine Zueck-Watkins

PHOTO IMAGING
Jolene McHugh

CONTRIBUTING EDITORS
Dan Golden
Pam Richter
Kathy Sullivan

INTELLECTUAL PROPERTY MANAGER
Michelle Gullett

PRINT & PRODUCTION COORDINATORS
Pat "Murphy" Benoit
Wayne Harty

DIRECTOR OF MARKETING
Rich Warren

EXECUTIVE EDITOR
Mike Reilly

PRESIDENT AND PUBLISHER
Terry Kroeger

Special thanks to Dawn Ream, director of marketing at Omaha's Henry Doorly Zoo & Aquarium, who went above and beyond to help produce the book.

Emmet is a Destination Nation stuffed animal, used with permission of Aurora World Inc. of Pico Rivera, Calif.

Photo reprints are available from the OWHstore. Call 402-444-1014 to place an order or go to OWHstore.com.

Omaha World-Herald Co.
1314 Douglas St. Omaha, NE 68102-1811
First Edition ISBN: 978-0-692-31051-9
Printed by Walsworth Publishing Co.
Marceline, MO